BLUE MOON

BLUE MOON

My Life in Verse

Margaret Ann Fuller

The poems in this book bring to life the wonderful mother
you are, together with the humour and sensitivity within
you. Thank you for everything – we are so proud.
With all our love, Kevin, David and Lisa

Poetry by Margaret Fuller

My pen may write one single line,
Or capture from a passing thought
A phrase alone that is just mine,
A precious feeling gently caught.
Soon the words will quickly flow,
And so my verse begins to grow.

CONTENTS

THE BEACH.

The night is dark far beyond the sea,
The laps of the waves are hushed,
And no one stands on the beach but me.
Men fought a bloody battle here this day,
Once women bathed in the sea,
While children ran by near at play.

Men encouraging one unto the other,
Who are these corpses here I see,
Is this my friend could that have been his brother?
Which are the defenders, and who the foe,
Who is left to point the finger where the condemnation
stands?
At dawn did they envisage what this night would bring?
Their enthusiasm now soaked into the sands.

I stand enraptured here to see before me,
Generations lost, are some to be engulfed and taken by
the sea,
Maybe in their silent sleep to each other
No more hate shall be born,
And they may awake refreshed in their far horizon
By a brighter dawn.

Am I the solitary victor, do I live to personify each man?
As a tidal wave shall forever splash,
And shall I stand immortal for another generation to
see, or
Will I in the course of time turn to ash?
Why is the moon afraid this night to shine?
As if an interloper here?
Or is the smoke from a hundred guns manipulated on
this day
Still in the air too thick to clear?

Shall I go forth and strive, and try to emulate just one?
Who gave his life for glory, or an unborn now
forgotten son,
Can I evacuate myself from here, or is this to be my
judgment
Day upon this foreign land,
And others in their turn may come and tread this soil that
We have freed, and I too shall be forgotten
And sink into the sand.

November 1970.

REMEMBERING.

I walked in a garden and remembered
A summer long since past.
Where in my youth time seemed endless,
And sunshine just to bask –
Away the hours of innocence on soft clovered lawns.
Do the birds sing as sweetly now?
As on those long lost dawns.
Days when all the good things were hesitant to leave,
Where gentle breezes coaxed petals from roses,
that lingered on a September eve.

I remembered crystals that fell in place of rain,
They sparkled and diminished hopelessly in vain.
Do Daffodils still nod their heads, and thrushes sing,
their sad lament?
Were those treasured hours carved upon my heart
really heaven sent?
Or simply the sweet mysteries of youth,
Loaned to each of us until we are old enough
to learn the truth.

September 1971.

A CHILDS POEM, WAKING ON A WINTER'S MORN.

Chilly mortal so forlorn,
Waking on a winter's morn.
To the sight of crisp white snow,
Watching the birds as they come and go,
With the crumbs from yesterdays tea.
How sad for them that they are not we –
Who nestle down beneath the clothes,
And listens while the north wind blows.
That rattles the latch on the stable door.
The horse, she waits until the thaw,
The little mice, they run and play,
Within the warmth of the pile of hay.
It looks so cold outside to me,
I think I'll stay in bed until tea!

November 1972.

DUNGEON GHYLL.

My heart races with the thrill,
Of climbing up this craggy hill.
To reach the top and see the view.
A cascade of green a vivid hue.
Soft water flowing down the side,
Where little worn stones gently glide.

Crystal clear the water races,
Twigs and a branch it quickly chases.
Reaching every cranny and nook,
Thence to find its own little brook.
A drinking place for lamb and sheep,
Before they settle down to sleep.

4.6.73.

WESTMORLAND.

I climbed a hill as in a dream,
And gazed upon this mountainous scene.
I trembled with the sheer delight,
Of seeing such a wondrous sight.
The sun was bright, the air was still,
The sheep they grazed on the side of the hill.

I watched the becks that fed the lake,
A sight to make every nerve awake.
The hills, the trees,
The moss, the breeze,
Can this be England at its best?
Where the heart can think, and the mind can rest.

For peace and solitude are here,
The things we treasure and hold most dear.
A priceless gift — as free as the air,
A sight for each of us to share.
The weary traveller must surely stop,
And rest his body in this lakeland spot.

4.6.73.

THE ROBIN.

Little Robin soft and sweet,
I watched you when you came to eat –
The crumbs I threw upon the ground.
I watched without a movement or sound,
For fear I frightened you away,
When all I wanted was to say –
Sing to me a song little bird?
A shrill little chirp I would have heard,
But another sound chased you away,
Come back, and sing to me another day.

6.7.73.

THIRTY DAYS.

Thirty days have I just,
Td do the things that I must.
One calendar month, September or June,
Thirty dawns that will come too soon.

To capture each moment before its too late,
Try even now to appreciate.
Things that seemed unimportant before,
Reach for them quickly too soon they're no more.

Breathe in the cool air after rain,
How many times to be my pleasure again?
Things only visible to the eye,
Why must they end the moment we die?

Thirty days to prepare,
For what, for whom, for where?
Never to walk along the sea shore,
Or to talk with the one I adore.

So much beauty on this earth
Only now I know its worth.
Little birds that sing at dawn,
A. cosy fireside snug and warm.

So very many words to say,
With no time to wait for another day.
Each one more precious than the last,
Why do the hours slip by so fast?

Thirty days have I hence,
So little time for recompense.
Oh dear God, leave me behind,
Please somehow try to change your mind.

15.7.73.

COMMUTING.

They come like bees from the hive,
As soon as the office clocks strike five.
The ones that are fat and forty,
And those who are thin and haughty.
Carrying cases and bags too wide,
Or newspapers where they can hide their faces,
From all the different races.
Who clamour for the five forty two,
Each day from Waterloo.

There's Harriet James from Edgware,
Feeding her face with a pear.
And there's old Mr Smith who a very nice bloke,
Commutes each day from Basingstoke.
They sit on their dusty seats,
And the cad with the newspaper peeps —
at the girl in the red mini skirt.
While the man in the chequered shirt,
Tries to think of a six letter verb,
To finish his daily crossword.

All the rushing and tearing,
And no time for caring.
Makes those with their rolled umbrellas,
Extremely discontented fellows.
There's the radical chap,
With a child on his lap.
They came for a day at the Zoo,
And somehow lost Mother at Waterloo,
So these are the daily commuters,
Soon even they'll be replaced by computers!

13.10.73.

INVISIBILITY.

I cannot see you,
Yet I feel your passing.
I see the swaying of the trees, that you are blowing
with your forcefulness.
And yet I know you can coax in the gentlest of
ways a petal from a rose.
Quite suddenly with one swoop a newspaper
hurries away frightened by your invisibility.
Old ladies wrap their coats in fear of you,
While children run and laugh as you whip their faces.
At night when I am laying still I can no longer feel you.
It is then I listen to you singing
and whistling around the trees,
Then it is as if you were never there, the air is still,
and silence prevails.
Until you decide to come and play
your invisible game again.

20.10.73.

THE MESSAGE.

The little child was skin and bone,
She stood quite still and all alone.
Now overcome with grief and fright,
Such wisdom had this little mite.
She knew not how, she knew not why,
Children like her were born to die.

Her sad eyes begging with this plea,
"Please someone give some food to me".
For toys and games she had no need,
Her only thoughts were where to feed.
With outstretched hands she took the grain,
Knowing she could not come again.

She tipped some on her Mother's plate,
Sadly to find it was too late,
Too tired and weary now to weep,
For this poor woman — just silent sleep.
Too old this child for her tender years,
With no one left to wipe her tears.

Now as I throw away our bread,
I think about that child instead.
Of the utter waste, and all the greed,
It seems so little that they need,
Oh God, help us to realize,
The message in that young childs eyes.

26.10.73.

THE TEMPTRESS.

When I am sad and feeling low,
There is one place I care to go.
Where tranquillity and peace of mind,
Overwhelm the worries left behind,
I find some quiet abandoned beach,
Where everyday needs are out of reach.

I shed my shoes and so feel free,
To walk barefoot along by the sea.
To feel the wet sand under my feet,
Cooling me from the suns strong heat.
Sometimes I walk for hours on end,
Beside this ever constant friend.

And when the sun has laid to rest,
That is the time I like the best.
For the stars come out and beckon me,
To bathe my body in the sea.
And as the waves caress the shore,
I feel their presence more and more.

Until at last I am her slave,
As I am engulfed by each new wave.
Nearer, nearer, calls the sea,
As if to court with me,
I see the ghosts of mariners of old,
She has consumed along with their gold.

As her waves come larger still,
Greater then becomes the thrill.
I walk out farther to her depths,
Like walking down some silken steps.
I'm mesmerised by her soft call,
As slowly then I start to fall.

While I am at her mercy now,
Something wakes me from her bowel.
I see the lighthouse gleaming bright,
Guiding the ships on this dark night.
Swiftly then I swim to the shore,
Knowing I'll return once more.

5.11.73.

THE ROAD SWEEPER.

He comes each day to clean the streets,
In worn out coat and grubby hat.
He talks to people that he meets,
About the weather, and this and that.
He has no friend to call his own,
Or place to think of as his home.

He stops a while to roll a fag,
Or raise his collar from the cold.
His job seems such a loathsome drag,
Particularly as he is so old.
The leaves are blowing from the heap,
Mocking him as he tries to sweep.

He sits on the steps of the village hall,
With a newspaper upon his knees,
And smiles at the children as they call,
While eating his lunch of bread and cheese.
He's always somewhere to be seen,
Keeping the streets so neat and clean.

When he is no longer here to sweep,
And the leaves fall, and the paper's scatter.
Will there be anyone who cares to weep,
Or will they think he does not matter.
I guess some folk will wonder why,
The streets are dirty as they pass by.

8.11.73.

CHANGING TIMES.

I used to think I lived in a village,
With buildings old and mellowed with age.
Where the trees blossomed in the spring,
And you could hear the church bells ring.
And freely park outside a shop,
No warden to tell you not to stop.
But alas, those days are gone,
Whatever was it that went wrong?

Now the developers have come to stay,
And slowly they're taking our beauty away.
It seems they crept in over night,
Now we are the victims — they won their fight!
One old house just had to go,
A Georgian beauty, don't you know!
They replaced it with that ghastly block,
Containing that big freezer shop.

Now they're starting on the road,
They say to ease the traffic load.
They proceeded then to fell the trees,
But did not stop there, if you please,
They moved Britannia on the green,
Now Esher's not a village scene.
Instead we are being turned around,
No longer a village — now a town.

One by one each old shop, where we could go and
browse,
For a dress, or coat, or blouse.
The developers will soon replace,
With Estate Agents, Banks, and office space.
Whatever would Queen Victoria say,
If she came back to visit us today.
I think the term she would have used
Without a doubt — "We are not amused".

9.11.73.

THE EARTHQUAKE.

The ground opened like a big well,
And everything around was consumed.
To the people it was a living hell,
Many were missing, only to be entombed,
Others ran as fast as they could,
In their confusion they fought each other.
The bad pilfering from the good.
And a child lay crying for its dead Mother.

Yesterday it was a beautiful city,
Today, a ruin steeped in pity.

11.11.73.

ROYAL WEDDING.

The dawn broke in a majestic way,
On this royal wedding day.
All over England people rejoice,
For the Princess Anne, and the man of her choice.
Kings and Queens and heads of state,
In Westminster Abbey solemnly wait.

Cheering crowds line the streets,
As each Londoner gaily greets.
From the flower seller's outside City Hall,
To the builder's at work repairing Saint Pauls.
Hear the Abbey bells ring loud and clear,
For this the wedding of the year.

14.11.73.

LEAVES.

Leaves, they are falling everywhere,
Yet it seems spring was such a short while ago.
When the trees burst forth, and each branch had
young green leaves there.
Now nearly bare with not a thing to show —
But the odd shrivelled leaf, falling to the ground.
To be swept into a golden mound.

16.11.73.

THE SPINNER.

I watched a spider spin her web,
She chose the thinest silken thread.
And delicately worked her weave,
Such time she took, but she achieved —
The very finest pattern there,
Sheer beauty — and such loving care.
Went into this her latest home,
No place for a fly to ever roam.

When her task was finally through,
And she could rest with little to do
She watched now with such pride and glee,
For some little creature to come to tea.
Some insect she might trap this day,
Travelling along its weary way.
But alas, some greater being walked by,
And her home sadly vanished before her eye.

25.11.73.

WINTER.

The snow fell softly to the ground,
Covering the earth without a sound.
Making a quilt so pure and white,
To reflect the moon's brilliant silver light.
The lake shone now like mirrored glass,
Nature alone had painted this scene,
No man could equal or surpass,
Where God with his palate and brush had been.

No movement from the lake was heard,
Or flutter from a passing bird.
Quite soon the dawn would begin to break,
And life will come again to the lake.
An ethereal calmness lays all around,
From the snow capped hill, to the silver dale.
Where soon the hedge sparrow will search the ground,
And gently mark God's snow white veil.

25.11.73.

OH GENTLE LITTLE BUTTERFLY.

Oh gentle little butterfly,
I watched you as you passed me by.
And only God can tell me why,
Your life's so short before you die.
Such beauty in one little being,
Such delicateness that I am seeing.

You play beneath those coloured flowers,
Where you have danced for hours and hours.
Buddleia's and hollyhocks too, are your silken towers.
A place for you to shelter from the showers.
Until a swift breeze comes this way,
And suddenly blows you from where you stay.

1.12.73.

CHRISTMAS CHEER.

Where is the Christmas spirit and cheer?
Where has it gone? For there's none of it here.
All over town the shop lights are out,
And the streets are empty, there's no one about.
Now the trains have gone slow,
And the postmen don't know —
Where the next letter bomb,
Is going to come from.

The unions don't care as they shout and fight,
What chaos and distruction they have brought in sight.
A five day week is a thing of the past,
And the petrol and oil is running out fast.
Now ten thirty's the time the T.V. must go out,
And its Heath's phase three that its all about.
The one cheerful thing the newspapers claim,
Is that Burton and Taylor are together again.

20.12.73.

DARK VIGIL.

I hear you calling as I try to sleep,
While your solitary vigil cunningly you keep.
It seems I turn a thousand times,
Your lonely hoot only reminds —
Me just how long this night will be,
Before the dawn shows itself to me.

Now the windows thick black glaze,
Are covered with a misty haze.
I hear the rain so softly fall,
Competing with your piercing call.
The shadows dance and mock me so,
Oh how I wish this night would go.

Please change your haunt, you wise old Owl,
Find another place to prowl.
And now with the worries of the day,
Formost in my thoughts — I pray
that sleep will overcome me soon,
And peace will come into my room.

23.12.73.

REMEMBRANCE.

I watched the woman quietly kneel,
And lay the wreath beneath the cross.
A far cry from that Battlefield,
Where her dear one was sadly lost.
No more the sound of distant drums,
No more the men who fell with their guns.
They gave their lives for us, and yet,
Too easily we do forget.

There were the boys to young for war,
With life's full years ahead.
A better world they were fighting for,
Now so many of them are dead.
And while their loved ones sadly mourn,
Let's hope they've found their brighter dawn.
So many songs have gone unsung,
In praise of the battles they have won.

Now resting beneath some foreign soil,
Where the dust has settled on the ground.
For each gallant soldier's sweat and toil.
A single Poppy may be found.
On dale and hillside laid to rest,
Thousands of men of the very best.
Now with each year a greater yield,
Of Poppies grow in that Flanders field.

1.1.74.

THE BROTHERHOOD.

They come from every walk of life,
A Butcher, or a man of Law.
And although they've usually got a wife,
What its all about she's never sure.
For the one thing that is understood,
The secrecy of their Brotherhood.

Each month on every fourth Thursday,
They hurry from their place of work.
Rehearsing the lines that they must say,
You'd spot them in their clean white shirt.
Making sure that they arrive,
No later than Four Forty Five.

I've wondered what their cause is for,
And the secrets in that little black book.
They gather behind that big locked door,
If through the key hole I could look,
I guess I know what I would spy,
Their all Gin Drinkers on the sly!

25.1.74.

PRELUDE TO SPRING.

In February's chill damp air,
I hear a Blackbird sing.
Somehow it makes me more aware,
That soon it will be spring,

Yet all around is crisp white snow,
And nature lays so calm and still,
Quite soon the crocuses will show,
And bathe the silent.

And there before my eyes I see,
Although the snow may still appear.
The buds are showing on the tree,
Telling me that spring is near.

I hear the birds begin to call their mating song at last,
And where the stream froze in the fall,
I see the water's running fast.

For me there is no other land,
Where my feelings are the same.
As they are in England,
When the spring comes around again,

5.2.74.

Shall we say we've no regrets,
After you have gone.
Dare we say we can forget,
If it takes all summer long.
So easy now to bravely say,
I'll not miss you when you go away.

Yet if you put me to the test,
My heart would break a thousand ways.
Remembering only the very best,
Of those glorious treasured days.
They say with time the wound will heal,
It never does, when the love is real.

6.2.74.

THE CHILDREN.

Two children waiting by a wall,
Who really should'nt be there at all.
Their little lives seemed so complete,
Now altered by fate's sudden sweep.

What was the word they heard him say,
What was an orphan anyway?
Both much too young to understand,
And missing the touch of their Mother's hand.

Their tiny hearts beat fast and wild,
Their gentle faces sadly smiled.
Yesterday the warmth of home,
Today out in the world alone.

So many children, such big rooms,
Where bewilderment and sadness looms.
Hand in hand slowly led away,
For them a strange and lonely day.

A different life now lies ahead,
No Mother to wipe the tears they shed,
No Father to scold them when the're wrong,
Where they wondered had they gone.

No longer their own favourite plate,
Instead they had to patiently wait —
With others in a single line,
Holding their tears back all the time.

A boy of six, a girl of five.
Who has the right now to decide —
When those dreaded words are said,
That both their parents are now dead.

Now it seems there's no outlet,
But children very soon forget.
And as the years quickly pass them by,
They'll understand why people die!

They'll weather all the storms ahead,
And when at last their childhoods fled.
Maybe they'll have the strength to say,
Life's not been so bad along the way.

17.2.74.

There is one poem left in me,
And with my pen I set it free,
Each feeling my thoughts and I may share,
Are very clearly written there.
And the secrets I cannot define?
Are hidden between each crystal line,
And when at last my pen is through,
I'll leave my poem for all to view.

22.2.74.

A POETS DREAM.

I'll show you a quiet restful place,
Where the willows bow at the streams bent edge,
And dazzle the water with their grace.
As they mingle with the sharp green sedge.
Where the mossy grass like a velvet spread,
Stretches to cover the ground we tread.

I'll find you a spot where you may rest,
Where nature commands with eloquence there.
You watch a Thrush gently feather its nest.
While you pleasantly breathe in the country air.
Then wait as a Kingfisher comes this way,
And quietly observe as he stalks his prey.

Perhaps its not the Fountains of Rome,
Or the Pyramids along the Nile,
It means more to me, for its England, its home.
The world I may travel, and yet all the while,
My heart is in England, by that rippling stream,
Where the birds sing their song — tis a poets dream.

3.3.74.

PRIME MINISTER'S WIFE.

Prime Minister's wife,
A lonely life.
Standing serenely by his side,
Watching people taunt and chide.
Sharing the glory and the falls,
Waiting in those draughty halls.
While others monopolise his soul,
Bravely playing your eloquent roll.

Prime Minister's wife,
A difficult life.
Smiling when you may feel sad,
Those occasions when your glad —
to have a weekend on your own,
Away from this your temporary home.
Commanding others admiration,
While sharing your life with the nation.

9.3.74.

FRIENDSHIP.

Friendship does not show —
In a gentle caress or kiss.
Or in those eyes that always glow,
By the knowledge of a lovers nearness.
It is not written in words of love,
Or hidden in the stars above.

Its there to soothe a troubled brow,
So each small gesture cannot fail,
For by its presence it helps somehow.
Not fashioned from a romantic tale,
But firmly shown by a clasping hand,
Or the comfort of one who understands.

Friendship comes in the strangest ways,
But once attained is always there,
And if perturbed when tempers fray,
These are the times you're more aware.
That a bond is sealed and you will find,
Its the hardest thing to leave behind.

12.3.74.

BOUND FOR THE MOON!

Midst a galaxy of stars,
Far away with Venus, and Mars.
Were three astronauts from Earth,
Where God had given them birth.
Travelling fast like a shining orb,
So much to see, and to absorb.
With Aurora, Goddess of the morning,
As her quivering lights were dawning.
Three men prepared for doom,
Three astronauts bound for the Moon!

On and on their space ship floats,
In that vacuum alone and remote.
With meteorites and asteroids,
They share that lifeless void.
Reflected by the Sun's strong light,
Like dust or rock passing in their sight.
Weightless in an unknown sphere,
With little time to think of fear.
God willing they will be there soon,
Three astronauts bound for the Moon!

17.3.74.

RAIN.

The tantalising sound of rain,
Beating on the window pane.
Failing quickly from the sky,
Giving life to earth thats dry.
Making pools like shining glass,
Splashing people as they pass.

The stimulating sound of rain,
Running fast down gutter and drain.
Playing havoc with the sun,
To tempt a rainbow to come.
Making cobwebs glisten and shine,
Swelling grapes upon the vine.

The rhythmic sound of rain,
Pelting down on hill and plain.
Or changing to a misty drizzle,
Leaving drops as clear as crystal,
And when the weathers close and warm,
Turning to a thunder storm.

20.3.74.

THE VISITOR.

It was autumn time when we first met,
She came to my back door,
Her fur was matted, dull, and wet,
And although I'd never met her before,
She let me stroke her thin frail form,
And purred when I brought her into the warm.

Then with each passing day,
I watched the life return to her,
And in her strange feline way,
She thanked me with her friendly purr,
For admittance to her new found home,
From where she came I've never known.

She stayed with me all winter through,
Sometimes she'd hide beneath a tree,
Watching the birds that came in view,
But never straying far from me,
She found a place within my heart,
I guess she knew that from the start.

It was early summer when she died,
Laying limp no longer aware of me,
Found there along the wayside,
I buried her beneath that tree,
And now the leaves have covered the ground,
Where peacefully she sleeps beneath a golden mound.

24.3.74.

TOO LATE.

I watched you gather violets for my grave,
Your heart was heavy as you gently laid —
a cluster on the fresh damp earth,
Such emotions have little worth,
Now my life is spent.
Too late for time to repent.
There were days I needed words,
And gentleness, your silence was unheard.
Now death has dulled my morning light,
And memories fast fading out of sight,
But the violets are fresh and sweet,
Although little comfort for the tears you weep.

30.3.74.

FOR DAVID.

Bathed in a childs grubby hand,
A little feathered being lay.
Lost in nature's wonderland,
As its last breath slipped away.

The boy handled it with care,
No thoughts of fun or play,
For death had made him more aware,
Cradling the bird found by the roadway.

He walked within the churchyard,
And gently buried it by the wall,
Knowing God would always stand guard,
Over creatures big and small.

God, watches over such as they,
Who help others along the way.
And when they cross the great divide,
The gates of heaven are open wide.

12.4.74.

SWEET LIFE.

Some say our lives are like the seasons,
As the buds burst in the depth of spring.
We — no time for patience or for reason.
Fledglings, like the new born birds that sing,
When summers of our youth seemed long,
Now too soon those years have gone.

As in autumn, rich golds appear,
And tolerance and kindness shows,
With winter slowly drawing near,
So our heart and spirit mellows,
And as the sands of time run fast,
We rejoice in the memories that will last.

Until at last our life is spent,
Too late to capture the seasons that went.

12.4.74.

A TREE.

I watched your branches bend and bow,
To God, as only you know how.
In winter when their stripped and bare,
Folk look on you with little care,
For whatever beauty can there be,
In a leafless, naked tree?

Then after winter's final flush,
Life within you begins its rush.
As inwardly you start to grow,
Where on each branch small buds will show,
And before a month of spring has passed,
Your beauty has appeared at last.

Then with July's hot summer days,
Your leaves lay in a thousand ways.
Like lace so delicately splayed,
For us to shelter in their shade,
Or birds to rest on hidden boughs,
Feeding on insects that they house.

When finally autumns drawing near,
And precious golds on you appear.
For now you've come into your own,
Like a king crowned on a throne.
Then what other sight can there be,
To equal the beauty of a tree!

27.4.74.

SUMMER DAYS.

How bright the morning sun,
Freed from winter's chains,
Shines down on everyone.
Where not a glimpse remains,
Of cold December days,
And young birds fly with little care,
Through the clearing morning haze.
Finding grubs, and insects where —
The dew has brought them from the ground,
And moles find comfort in their mound.

As the sun gives life to plants,
And buds are coaxed to open wide,
Encouraging bees to hover and dance,
And capture the nectar hidden inside.
Then bent and wilted a slender flower,
With no protection from the heat,
Is soon revived by a gentle shower.
As a butterfly makes her retreat,
Beneath the petals of a rose,
Slowly carried with the breeze that blows.

As the day draws to an end,
In this early month of May,
As summer's glory now ascends,
And fallen blossom is brushed away,
The evening sky is clear and warm.
Where giant petunias scent the air,
Their petals closing until dawn.
Then calm and peace is everywhere,
But for the calling of a bird,
Not another sound is heard.

22.5.74.

THOUGHTS OF A
BORED HOUSEWIFE.

If I were free like a bird,
I'd leave this complicated nest,
Without a whimper or a word.
To do the things I like the best,
Forget my obligations,
And those in — laws and relations.

Find some far off foreign shore,
Where time does not exist,
Meet a man I could adore,
Do the things I can't resist,
Then I'd take a jet to Rome,
With no thoughts of going home.

When I'm tired of window shopping,
And bored with pink champagne,
I'd then decide to drop in,
On some Arab's rich domain.
To be bathed in milk and honey,
Cossetted with love and money.

Then make tracks for Monte Carlo,
To play the spinning wheel,
As I watch the money grow,
I'll then know how it feels,
To be rich and independent,
And so very glad I went.

Before my dream is through,
I'll buy myself a boat,
With sixteen lovers for the crew,
For one whole year we'd stay afloat,
And sail the seven seas,
To return just when we please.

But alas, its just a dream
Of a bored and lonely housewife,
And though exciting it may seem.
It could never be my life,
For instead I've got the chores,
And those extremely crashing bores!

30.5.74.

WHY.

With her in her waking hours,
The sheer uncertainty of death.
Waiting as the growth devours,
To consume her final breath.
Seeking promises of life,
As she questions – WHY.
Feeling no longer woman or wife,
Watch her slowly die.

8.6.74.

LOVE,

Bravely blossoms in the heart,
And shows in many beautiful things.
A single rose, a cherished hour.
The colours that a sunset brings.
If separation sadly parts —
those lovers in their leafy bower,
Like angels lost in their flight above,
Their wings are forever touched with Love.

13.6.74.

WITHOUT A SOUND.

Watch him walking out of the door.
Is this the man you used to adore?
Turn away for he will not wave.
Shut your eyes for her will not see.
Gone — his smoke and after shave.
All that is left is your dignity,
And the pieces scattered on the ground,
Pick them up without a sound.

16.6.74.

THE LIZARD.

So many have stood and watched in awe,
At the beauty of this Cornish shore.
Where the rollers break on the granite rock,
At the Lizard — on England's most southerly spot,
Where the wheeling gulls give their screeching cry
As they flock to the cliffs, and circle and fly —
With the wind as it battles against the sea.

Where far beyond the beacons glow,
The little ships bravely come and go,
And the gleaming lighthouse stands to warn,
Them of the fog, or an oncoming storm,
With her searching light she scans the foam,
And guides each little ship safely home.
Away from the perils of the treacherous sea.

26.6.74.

THE SEA.

See the great rollers sweep into the bay,
Swirling in fury as they come from the sea.
Lapping the shore with their salty spray.
From the headland and cove along to the quay.

Watch the driftwood float onto the beach,
Bits from barges and broken sails,
Once out at sea — now their in your reach,
The remains of so many storms and gales.

Hear the mournful call of the sea,
Controlled by the Moon for the turn of her tide.
Like a sorrowful woman she cries to me,
As she shelters the thousands who braved her and died.

27.6.74.

THE TWILIGHT HOURS.

When caught between those twilight hours,
And sleep has slowly drifted away.
Lost with all her mystic powers,
In the confusion of another day,
When fears and shadows flood your mind,
To penetrate your every thought,
You toss and turn but only find,
Each hour has left you more distraught.
When trapped within that dark despair,
Before the night gives way to the dawn,
You seek a gleam of hope somewhere,
The promise of a golden morn.

You pray the night will soon be spent,
And the anguish and the fear relent.

Quite soon the new day will be born,
As slowly the darkness slips away.
Like the sudden clearing in a storm.
A calmness comes as you quietly lay,
And watch the dawn break in the sky.
Like magic the birds begin their song,
As they leave their nests and swiftly fly
Beyond the glow of the new horizon.
Hear the thrush and blackbird's lilting tune,
While the fears that consumed the night,
Slowly disappear from your room,
Leaving the warmth of the morning light.

29.6.74.

DUST.

Its all the same in the end —
Everything will turn to dust.
Things that beautifully blend,
Others drastically attacked by rust.
A flower, or a little moth.
Mansions full of priceless wares.
A solid oak, a piece of cloth,
All nature's beauty that we share.

Our bodies through the years,
Full of knowledge and of learning,
With death bring others tears,
And loneliness and yearning.
Such reasoning seems wrong,
Yet life, a repetition of all things.
To be replaced as soon as it has gone,
Each dawn another bird will sing.

Can it then be said —
Our lives begin within the grave,
And those who lay there are not dead,
But silently the wretched and the brave,
Are mocking us who dare to pity those,
Who leave their crumbling bodies in disgust.
Invisible, yet life that never goes,
For spirits cannot turn to dust.

24.7.74.

MEUDON COVE.

Watch the sea racing from its depths,
To meet the rugged Cornish shore.
Frothy white horses reaching the sky,
Gigantic in their height and breadth.
Swirling, leaping, with a piercing roar.
Mocking the gulls and their screeching cry,
That circle and swoop on the desolate beach,
Beating their wings against the inshore gale,
As they carry their prey to the cliffs out of reach, Finding
shelter in the hard Cornish shale.

Hear the wind as she whips the sand,
Making mounds against the rocky edge,
To be washed back with the next full tide.
Leaving a stark beauty from shore to headland,
White against the black crumbling ledge.
See a cormorant swiftly ride,
On the crest of an in coming wave,
As she braves the fury of the sea,
That has taken many mariners to their grave,
When their ships have missed the Helford quay.

26.7.74.

LOOKING THROUGH
A TINTED GLASS.

Looking through a tinted glass,
With all the rainbows dazzling glow.
At memories of a childhood passed.
How vividly they come and go.
Pictures of those summer days,
Where time was lost in endless fun,
And the future seemed a far off maze.
To us whose life had just begun.

Where every crystal raindrop seemed
The largest we had ever seen,
And butterflies with wings that gleamed
Of the brightest red, and blue, and green,
And all those characters portrayed
Within the pages of our mind,
Came to life with every game we played,
But how quickly we left it all behind.

27.7.74.

WATERGATE.

He stood obsessed with worldly power,
While others suffered his misdemeanour,
And unconsciously lost his finest hour,
To live a lie, this fanatical schemer.
A President lost in a whirlpool of greed,
With his future held on a reel of tape.
Forced in the end to bow down and concede,
To the shame and disgrace of Watergate.
In his closing years he may learn to repent,
Will he realize then what democracy meant?

15.8.74.

AUGUST.

The street outside is wet with rain,
Soon it will be September again,
And the last rose will perish and fall.
Leaving practically nothing at all
of a summer nearly spent,
Where fallen petals frail and bent,
Turn to dust beneath our feet,
As August makes her slow retreat.

The birds begin their endless flight,
To distant lands far out of sight,
And butterflies and insects dare
to rest contentedly aware,
In foliage green and overgrown,
Where summer flowers now full blown,
No longer rise to greet the sun,
For autumn has at last begun.

27.8.74.

Are those the ashes of our love?
Dismembered fragments on the ground.
Now winter's chill has touched your heart,
No glimmer of love is to be found —
in your eyes or with your smile.

12.9.74.

A home is a glimpse into ones personality.
A garden is a place of surprises,
An ever changing picture of tranquillity.

EPITAPH.

She cannot speak or lift her frame,
Nor smell the scent of these purple flowers,
That shroud her final small domain,
Perhaps these are her finest hours,
For she cannot rise to wipe their tears,
Or greet their morning Sun,
And if they call she never hears,
For her death has just begun.

23.9.74.

I WONDER WHY.

Some days I wake, and wonder why
Mortals such as we are blessed,
With the daylight in the sky,
And darkness when we need to rest.

I'll never really understand,
What is the magic of the brain,
That makes the movement in our hand.
Or how the blood flows through each vein.

Some days I wake, and wonder why
The ground is fresh with morning dew.
How easily a bird can fly,
What makes a summer sky so blue.

I've often watched in winter time,
The softly falling white snowflakes.
No draughtsman ever could design,
Such intricate, yet perfect shapes.

Some days I wake, and wonder why
The chemistry of life is such,
It makes a new born baby cry,
Or a lover to respond to touch.

Though given all these many things,
At times we're discontented,
We disregard the joy life brings,
By taking everything for granted.

2.10.74.

Remarkable how love can wane,
Too soon the passion disappears,
And foolish words are said in vain,
When hopelessly we hide our tears.

———————-———————

Will strength support my feeble heart?
When love has slipped away.
Will words of comfort play their part?
When fond emotions stray.

22.10.74.

Dare I drift into the night of dreams?
And let my spirit float beyond the veil of day,
Where subconsciously we dwell in earthless schemes. In
a game that only dreamers play.

Once I recall a vision came to me,
Beckoning with outstretched arms,
Her face I could not see,
Nor could I touch her spirit that the night embalmed.

Who are they, who share that priceless gift,
Of sublime peace and solitude,
Beyond the barrier of the moonlit mist,
Sometimes to glimpse a rare and spiritual interlude.

Perhaps I shall not drift, or dream, or see,
again, that ethereal vision that came to me before,
A premonition of the ghost of me,
That quite by chance I saw.

                                        27.10.74.

ESMERALDA BEDINGTON.

FOR MY DAUGHTER.

LISA.

ESMERALDA BEDINGTON.

Through the tall impressive gate,
Came the coach in regal state.
Although the journey had been long,
Miss Esmeralda Bedington,
Viewed the splendour of the place,
With a smile upon her face.
Past the courtyard and the clock,
Past the vine and stable block.
She saw the statues tall and fine,
"To think that all of this is mine".
Thought Esmeralda Bedington.

At last the house was to be seen,
Flanked with lawns of velvet green,
With marble steps, just twenty four,
And the largest solid oak front door.
On either side were grecian urns,
Full of the most exotic ferns,
And standing in a single row,
Was everyone she ought to know.
The butler introduced each one,
What terribly exciting fun,
Thought Esmeralda Bedington,

1.

In the hallway vast and wide,
Were marble statues either side,
And tables made in marquetry.
So many precious things to see.
Priceless pictures on the wall,
Indeed this was the finest hall,
That anyone had ever seen,
The carpet was the palest green,
And as she stepped upon the stairs,
The footmen stood each side in pairs,
For Esmeralda Bedington.

The carpet was so very thick,
She was unable to be quick,
But when she reached the final stair,
The sight had caught her unaware.
Thirty doors from left to right,
With not a speck of dust in sight.
Two pair of footmen led her to,
The bedroom with the finest view,
When she saw what was inside,
Her eyes they opened very wide.
Oh Esmeralda Bedington.

2.

Mirrors hung from wall to wall,
And the windows were so frightfully tall,
With quite the deepest violet drapes,
Held in place with golden tapes,
She opened up a cupboard door,
And hung in covers to the floor,
Were rows and rows of silken dresses,
And to tend her golden tresses,
On the dressing table there,
Were silver brushes for the hair,
Of Esmeralda Bedington.

The butler knocked upon the door,
Standing there with cakes galore,
And tea upon a silver tray.
"His Lordship", he did say,
"Waited in the drawing room",
"And hoped he would see madam soon".
She thanked him for his curtesy,
And said she'd see him after tea,
She poured her tea with lots of cream,
"Oh what a lovely day its been",
Said Esmeralda Bedington.

3.

She tossed her shoes into the air,
She sat upon the satin chair.
In the pocket of her cloak,
She found that very precious note,
From Lady Connington Desquire,
Written to her to enquire,
If she would wed her brother Claude,
Who'd returned of late from abroad,
Her stately home of Milton Kerr,
She promised as a gift to her,
Miss Esmeralda Bedington.

She wrote and said she would be pleased,
If this opportunity she seized,
To take the hand of Connington Desquire,
And that she would really require,
Or so her letter did infer,
To own the house of Milton Kerr,
And so at last she came to view,
Her house and her suiter too,
Now sitting in her mauve boudoir,
The heart was filled with love and fire,
Of Esmeralda Bedington.

4.

She chose the dress with silken thread,
She pinned some jewels upon her head,
She found the finest satin shawl,
And viewed the mirror on the wall.
"I'm quite the prettiest of girls",
"I think I'll wear those double pearls".
Now dressed and ready for her match,
She lifted up the heavy latch,
And crossed the corridor to go,
Down to the drawing room below.
Miss Esmeralda Bedington.

She glided down the spacious stairs,
She saw the footmen in their pairs.
Past the statues in the hall,
Past the paintings on the wall,
She put her satin shawl in place,
And forced a smile upon her face.
Perhaps a trifle insecure,
For now she'd reached the big white door.
The butler waited for a while,
And then announced in gracious style,
Miss Esmeralda Bedington.

5.

She cast her eyes into the room,
To be struck with sudden gloom,
She heard the clock begin to chime,
She saw the footmen serving wine,
And sitting on a silver chair,
With quite the longest, reddest hair,
And for sure the oldest face.
Oh what a terrible disgrace,
Was Lord Connington Desquire,
With not a feature to inspire,
Miss Esmeralda Bedington.

"Oh what a disaster this has been",
"He's quite the ugliest man I've seen".
He has big ears, he has no teeth",
"The sight of him fills me with grief.
Without a word she left the room,
She asked the butler if the groom
would bring the coach and horses too.
"To look at him makes me so blue",
"I could not possibly have wed",
"I really would rather be dead".
Said Esmeralda Bedington.

6.

She left the house in such a state,
For she could not bear to wait.
Past the statues tall and fine,
"Now they never would be mine".
Past the vines and stable block,
Past the courtyard and the clock.
Softly crying to herself,
"I'd rather be left on the shelf".
"For he was an awful sight",
And so she vanished in the night,
Miss Esmeralda Bedington.

The End.

3.11.74.

7.

TO A DYING FRIEND.

How we tried to hide from you,
The sadness that we felt.
Wondering if you really knew,
The cruel blow fate had dealt.

I wanted not to look —
Upon your gaunt enquiring face,
Where once such animation beamed.
Now pain and anguish has replaced,
The hopes and promises you dreamed.

We tried to say — before we left,
So many things to comfort you,
But words of comfort seemed bereft,
For somehow your eyes told us you knew.

I wanted not to look —
But to remember the Pat I knew.

4.12.74.

THE LAKE.

The icicles cling to the tips
Of each cascading branch.
Caught in the water's grips.
As December's frost enchants,
Where swan and mallard glide,
On this silver looking glass,
To the banks on the other side,
And rest in the crystal grass.

As the misty moonlight gathers
To dance on each willow and beech,
Where even the stately firs,
Hang heavy and silently reach
To the ground with the weight of the snow,
And the birds nestle and wait,
Neath the moon with its heavenly glow,
For the dawn to appear on the lake.

14.12.74.

The sweetest sound I ever heard
Was on a bleak mid winter day.
The singing of a little bird.
I think that God sent him to say
Spring would soon be on its way.

18.12.74.

IN VAIN.

Bombs left in pillar boxes, or
underneath and inside cars.
In a departmental store,
And others placed in crowded bars,
Where innocent lives are taken in vain,
And others suffer anguish and pain.

I'm sure God never intended
a Cristian to walk with a gun.
Or a child to be born and bred,
To look upon killing as fun,
Or to live with fear each day,
Knowing only violence at play.

Where Catholics and Protestants alike,
With their hands on the butt of a gun.
Mock their religion to fight,
But no victory will ever be won,
And the bloodshed will have been in vain,
For both Protestants and the Sinn Fein.

22.12.74.

BLACKBIRD.

Blackbird, by my window sill,
Your gay song brings me cheer.
Flowing from your yellow bill,
The sweet sound that I hear.

Before the day is hardly born,
Where from my bed I listen for
That sound that greets the dawn,
And pleases me once more.

1.1.75.

MISHANDLING.

Happiness, I know not why
your presence is not here.
Why you ignore the tears I cry.
When seldom you appear

I know no words to say.
I know not how my heart will cope.
I hesitate and turn away.
Such moments filled with joy and hope

Are not given to destroy,
By lack of understanding.
With these tactics I employ,
My happiness, is lost with such mishandling.

12.1.75.

CELLULOID WOMAN.

Celluloid woman that you are,
Insecure in all your trappings.
Those who know you from afar,
Never look beneath your wrappings.
Never wonder what you feel.
Now is the time for taking stock,
For there's a part of you thats real,
And soon you're for the chopping block.

18.1.75.

DISCARDED.

Discarded and worn a Victorian chair,
Hidden away from the daylight's glare.
Where years of dust had encrusted her,
In a coat of soft grey fur.
Where spiders nestled in each fold,
Of the shredded damasks faded gold.
And spun their intricate fine webs,
Around her gracefully carved legs.

Once ladies sat upon this chair,
Caught up in many a gay affair.
Bejewelled in all their finery,
Sitting talking, or taking tea.
What stories I wonder could she tell,
Of the better times she knew so well.
Now forgotten in the attics gloom,
Once the pride of the Drawing room.

18.1.75.

TO MY LOVE.

Our love was:
The thrill of our first kiss.
The tingling down my spine.
The partings, and the bliss
Of knowing you were mine.
The ring you gave to me,
For all the world to see.

Our love is:
The friendship deep and lasting,
Now the passions flown.
The happiness you bring,
And the pleasures we have known.
The contentment that we share,
With our lasting love affair.

5.2.75.

ILKLEY MOOR.

When I returned to Ilkley Moor,
Twas as if I'd never been away.
For all was as it had been before.
Each patch of gorse, each mound of clay.
All my years of past endeavour
Seemed of little consequence,
Where in the distance stretching forever,
That rugged beauty, that vast expanse.

No humbler being could have stood alone,
With wind and rain upon their face,
And not have felt the peace I've known,
When fact and fiction interlace,
And all those years that passed with youth,
To seek ambition, and wealth galore,
And yet if I could speak the truth,
My wealth was there on Ilkley Moor.

7.2.75.

LITTLE DAUGHTER.

Little daughter mine,
These wishes are for you,
A life of peace, that is combined
With love and understanding too.
I wish for you such happiness,
With strength to guide you through
The times of sadness and distress,
I hope that they'll be few,
Remember people matter most.

So be kind to those you meet
Less fortunate than you.
Be patient and discreet,
And smile when you are blue,
Don't sacrifice your years ahead,
With the foolish whims of youth.
Although your heart may rule your head,
Always learn to speak the truth,
Then joy I know will come to you.

12.2.75.

ILLUSIVE.

Silver white or crystal clear,
Hiding in the milky way.
First you're gone, and then you're here.
Such tantalising games you play.
I'm weary with continuous gaze,
Now a gleaming gold cocoon,
Soon lost behind a misty haze,
Illusive old man in the Moon.

13.2.75.

MOORGATE.

These were the people of yesterday
A mangled mass of human life.
Crushed together in heaps they lay.
Someone's brother, someone's wife.
Rushing not to be left behind.
An everyday crowd of sadness and laughter,
Down the steps to the Northern Line,
To be victims of the Moorgate disaster.
Now the're listening for a whimper or cry,
Where but for the grace of God, lay you or I.

4.3.75.

NO MORE.

No more I'll see the Willow
That sways within the breeze.
Or hear the shrill familiar call,
Of the Robin that says "Please
Remember me, remember me,
Some tit bits for my tea".

No more I'll walk along the path
And gather each dead bloom,
Of this years crop of roses
That scented every room,
In the decade that has flown,
For soon I'll leave this home.

And with it will remain,
A chapter of my life,
Of both sad and happy days,
As a mother and a wife.
The children's laughter, and their tears,
That echoed through the years.

Will haunt each lonely room,
And when we've packed and gone.
Will they care for you the same?
Will you wonder what is wrong?
When their Dog scratches at your door,
And the Robin comes no more.

8.5.75.

JONES.

Although his parents pride and joy,
Jones was quite the ugliest boy.
With glasses perched upon his nose,
And pimples from his head to toes.
It was not his idea of fun,
To find himself in a Rugby Scrum.
Feeling quite superior to
The other fellows that he knew.
On one particular fateful day,
He found he had a game to play.

His colleagues waiting on the field,
'What joy to them this game would yield'.
For this was just their chance to show,
Jones exactly where to go.
Viewing with their coupled heads,
The position of his spindly legs,
With baited breath and hopes held high,
They kicked the ball into the sky.
Full back Jones with dimmed eyesight,
Realised the anguish of his plight.

Inprisoned there within the ruck,
He thought 'What terribly hard luck'.
Sad of heart, — the ball now gone,
Whatever was it that went wrong?
With bleeding head, and bleeding knee,
He ran as far as he could see.
To the corner of the Rugby pitch,
Suffering now the most terrible stitch.
Feeling sad and all alone,
Wishing that he was at home.

Suddenly with such surprise,
The ball appeared before his eyes.
This was his one and only chance,
Making a most dramatic prance,
Fifty yards up to the line,
From head to foot in dirt and grime.
He succeeded then to score a try,
Giving out a most hearty cry.
At last good luck had come his way,
He was now hero of the day!

22.9.75.

THE OVERSEER.

Such patience lies within that tree,
Where majestic in its solitude
It towers over you and me.
Sturdy branches now protrude,
Once the shoots of a yesteryear.
Now calmly reaching to the sky,
Looming like an overseer,
Swaying with the breeze on high.

October winds have stripped you bare,
Naked like an ancient shrine,
Your golden leaves lay everywhere.
The compost of another time.
New seasons bring their different charms.
Winter snows protect the shoots
Cradled in your crooked arms,
Feeding from your tangled roots.

Yet from one very small acorn,
This solid English Oak was born.

26.9.75.

FALLING LEAVES.

The falling leaves in autumn shades,
Of crimson red, or mottled gold.
Float from the trees in gentle waves
To rest in heaps ten thousandfold.

30.10.75.

DYING EMBERS.

The last dying embers
Flicker in the grate.
The moments one remembers,
Like the flames evaporate.
Soon the ashes of the old year
With our dreams of yesterday,
Will be raked and disappear,
And our dreams will slip away.

28.12.75.

THE EARLY HOURS.

Sometimes I wake in the early hours
And watch the dawn appear.
I listen for the blackbird
His song I love to hear,
But when the winter wind
Beats on my window pane,
I wonder if I'll ever hear
My blackbird sing again.

6.1.76.

THE BLACK CAT.

His lithe body stalked between the shrubs,
In the heat of a summer's day.
Birds searching for tiny grubs
Quickly flew away,
With the threat of sudden danger,
As the cat, black and sleek,
Nestled beneath a blue hydrangea,
Prepared to wait, one hour, one week?

Cautiously the birds returned to their habitat,
His eyes now half closed in shallow sleep.
They did not realise the quickness of a cat.
For with just one swift leap,
He held a sparrow captive in his paws,
Suddenly the peace of their sanctuary was disturbed,
As they witnessed the death between his claws
Of yet another unsuspecting bird.

1.2.76.

EMBRACE.

There is a sadness as the winter ends,
When birds no longer need us
For their friends.
Slowly from hill to vale the nucleus
Of winter, is lost within the birth,
Of another new born spring.
Where movement beneath the hardened earth,
Is but a glimmer of new life's happening.

It was the other week we briskly walked,
Beside the frozen lake,
Where swarms of moorhens squawked
And cursed the ice they could not break.
Now the scent of spring is in the air,
And we no longer walk with quickened pace,
But observe the beauty everywhere,
As winter and spring gently embrace.

28.2.76.

CAT AND MOUSE.

Today the mouse is dead.
Yesterday he ran and frolicked
On the flower bed.
Beneath Primulas, and Polyanthus leaves;
He played his merry game.
Now he neither sleeps nor breathes;
Or frolics in the Sun.
The cat made sure of that,
With his ten minutes of fun.

14.3.76.

AN ENGLISH GARDEN,

DEDICATED TO BEVERLY NICHOLS.

Slowly above the tree tops high,
Where lark and swallow greet the dawn.
The shimmering rays of an indigo sky.
Iridescent blues softly cluster to form
The start of a summer's day.
As spring quietly slips away.

When afternoons are times to laze
Beneath the willow's spreading boughs,
To the living pond we silently gaze,
And now and then we nod and drowse,
As we sip our glass of rich red wine,
While bees settle on the columbine.

The buddleia sways with the barmy breeze,
And startles each dormant butterfly.
We gather our thoughts at times like these,
And contemplate the reason why!
Such healing powers can be derived,
From both garden, and from countryside.

As the silver leaves on the birches quiver,
Small birds search the ground for grubs
Then fly to their nests, their wares to deliver.
I see somewhere amongst the shrubs,
My black cat stirs to lick a paw,
Then settles down to sleep once more.

There is joy in an English garden,
On a long summer's day.
It is the place to find contentment when
Hope and strength seems far away.
For nowhere in the world you'll find,
Such freedom and such peace of mind.

24.4.76.

A FLICKER OF YOUTH.

How many years have you known?
That have casually slipped away?
In seconds the hours have flown
Taking with them a year in a day.
Leaving memories far from the truth
Just a glimpse of a flicker of youth.

You say you remember your childhood,
Like spring the grass was so green,
But I wonder would you if you could,
Return to that far away scene.
To live your life through once again,
I think it would not be the same.

For the journey has mellowed your mind,
And the passing of time is a mirage,
We seek but rarely do we find,
Beneath such a vast camouflage,
The joys that we knew in the past,
For such moments so rare never last.

8.6.76.

LITTLE BLACK JASPER.

Little black Jasper curled up by my door.
My friend forever, constant and sure.
With bright Topaz eyes, two jewels in the night.
Nocturnal creature, mice flee from your sight.
Such delicate patterns on ledges and floors,
Made with the print of your muddy black paws. Always
washing your sleek shiny coat.
Regal you stand, alone and remote,
Yet somehow I know you always will be,
There when I need your quiet company.

1.11.83.

Library of Congress Control Number:		2018912467
ISBN:	Hardcover	978-1-5434-9301-6
	Softcover	978-1-5434-9300-9
	eBook	978-1-5434-9299-6

Print information available on the last page.

Rev. date: 11/13/2018

To order additional copies of this book, contact:
Xlibris
800-056-3182
www.Xlibrispublishing.co.uk
Orders@Xlibrispublishing.co.uk
782901